Adventures with God

What is faith?
Faith is seeing 'through the veil';
it's encountering the presence
of a heavenly dimension
within, around and underneath
our everyday world
and being warmed by
the Love we discover there.

By the same author:

Fiction

The White Gates Adventures:
The Kicking Tree
Ultimate Justice
Wind and Wonders
The Spark

The Flip trilogy:
On the Edge
Beyond the Horizon
The Daisychain

Non-fiction

WYSIWYG Christianity : Young People & Faith in the Twenty-First Century

Podcasts

Our World - God's World
https://anchor.fm/trevor-stubbs

Adventures with God

Exploring faith and intimacy with infinite God.

TREVOR STUBBS

Copyright © 2020 Trevor Stubbs

The moral right of the author has been asserted.

Apart from any fair dealing for the purposes of research or private study, or criticism or review, as permitted under the Copyright, Designs and Patents Act 1988, this publication may only be reproduced, stored or transmitted, in any form or by any means, with the prior permission in writing of the publishers, or in the case of reprographic reproduction, in accordance with the terms of licences issued by the Copyright Licensing Agency. Enquires concerning reproduction outside those terms should be sent to the publishers.

The Listening People
15 Cleeve Grove
Keynsham,
Bristol, BS31 2HF

ISBN 978 0-9550100-7-1

British Library Cataloguing in Publication Data.
A catalogue record for this book is available from the British Library.

Standing in the midst of the Areopagus, Paul addressed the crowd.

"People of Athens, I can see you revere the gods in all things.

For, going through your city, I found among your shrines one dedicated to the Unknown God. It is he who I want to tell you about.

This very one, the God who made the world and everything in it, is lord of heaven and earth. He does not live in man-made temples. Nor does he need human hands to tend him as if he had need of anything. He is the one that gives life and breath and everything to us ...

... so that we should search for this Lord and maybe in some way, scrabbling about in our blindness, come to find him, although he is not far from any one of us."

Acts 17:22-25, 27

Before you begin...

'Why do you believe in God?' has been a question put to me all through my life as an Anglican clergyman. Some who have asked that have known quite well that I can't come up with scientific proofs or conclusive philosophical arguments. Even the cleverest minds have never been able to find of ways to prove God's existence.

Each of us has to decide whether or not we're going to search and explore for signs of God which surpass the ordinary ways of knowing something.

I enjoy the dry wit of Douglas Adams in his *Hitch Hiker's Guide to the Galaxy*; it is a masterpiece. But for Adams the idea of God is a distracting figment of the imagination that is always too small and ineffective and whose main purpose seems to be a source of income for those who profit from pilgrims on their quest to find of him.

Adam's hero, Arthur Dent, and his girlfriend, Fenchurch, go in search of 'God's Final Message to his Creation'. Eventually they come in sight of the thirty-foot-high letters on the side of the Quentulus Quazgar Mountain on a distant planet.

> *They gazed at God's Final Message in wonderment, and were slowly and ineffably filled with a great sense of peace, and of final and complete understanding.*
>
> *Fenchurch sighed, 'Yes,' she said, 'that was it.'*

The message turns out to be: 'We apologise for the inconvenience.' Adams believes that asking ultimate questions of 'life, the universe and every-thing', including God, is a pointless, unprofitable waste of time.

However, unlike Douglas Adams, I have discovered the quest to be one with a rich and exciting reward. I have been far from inconvenienced because I have come to know just a little of the stunning reality of God. I have come to the foot of the Quentulus Quazgar Mountain but have found the message to be quite different. It is, 'Seek and you will find'.

I believe in God because I believe I've met him, and he knows me. I can't prove that and I'm not even going to try. All I offer are a few ideas as an invitation for you to spend a little time in exploring the question.

You can explore alone or in small groups. If you are using this booklet in a group, then you might like to rearrange the readings and questions to suit your session rather than go through them in the order I have presented them.

You can use any bible translation but I recommend a modern version alongside your traditional one, if that's your preference. The everyday language of today can unlock doors on the journey. If you haven't come across it yet, you might find Eugene Peterson's *The Message* version worth a look.

1
Finding God in our Hearts

Anita and William meet up with a friendly married couple, Heather and Mike in a local park. Anita and William are planning to get married and they are quizzing their friends to get some tips about married life.

Anita: Didn't you get married in church, Heather?

Heather: Yes. St Mark's. We still go there.

Anita: Did you have to go to the church before you got married?

Heather: We had a 'qualifying connection', so didn't have to but we chose to.

William: God's kinda important to you, I guess.

Mike: Yes. Couldn't recommend him enough. Sorted us out a couple of times.

William: How'd you mean?

Mike: Things haven't always been plain sailing. Do you remember that time the firm I worked for went bust? It took several months to get a new job.

Anita: So, how'd God help? You still had to go through a difficult patch.

Mike: Sure, but if God's there – in your heart – then it makes all the difference.

Anita: How does that work, then? In your heart?

Heather: Well, he comes and lives in you. As simple as that. Guides you, helps you through... makes sure you don't feel alone sometimes.

Anita: Sounds a bit weird. Like some kind of alien creeping under the skin. Ugh...

Mike: (*Laughing.*) You've been watching too many sci-fi films, Anita. It's not like that at all. It's, like, he belongs there. He fits into a God-shaped space and kinda completes you.

Heather: And God *never* forces you into doing anything, ever. He guides but he doesn't take over – you've always got control. And, I guess, you can kick him out any time you want... But you wouldn't want, really. It's only in the times when you are tempted to do something you know he really wouldn't like that you think about shutting him out.

But then you know it's wrong. It's not like *he's* shouting at you from

	the inside; it's your own conscience that makes you realise.
Mike:	And then when you admit to going off track, he just seems to say. Glad you're back, so let's continue on forward. Like he's the best kind of friend, I guess.
William:	Friend? That sounds a bit corny. How can great almighty God be a friend? I can believe father, boss, leader but 'friend' seems rather too... I don't know.
Mike:	Familiar. Down to earth?
William:	Well, yes.
Mike:	But that's exactly what he is – down to earth. That's where Jesus comes in – a human being but also God himself. He's a friend. The best friend you could ever have. He called his disciples friends.
Anita:	That bit's the hardest bit to believe. I don't get how a human being could have been God.
Heather:	But God, being God, has the power to be born a human, hasn't he? And he *had* to do it. God had to leave behind all his heaven stuff and become one of us or he'd be forever 'out there'—
Mike:	While we suffer everything that can go wrong for humans as he just looks on, feeling sorry for us. That wouldn't be good enough for me.
William:	Or me.
Anita:	That's why he had to die on a cross, then? Face the dark bits.
Mike:	Exactly. If he hadn't done that, he would have been useless to me in that dole queue – or when my dad died.
Anita:	So the God who died on the cross is now alive inside you... and in everybody else who goes to church.
Heather:	Ah, well, no... Not exactly *everybody* in church. Anybody can attend – they don't have to be God-centred people. Some of them go for all the wrong reasons – some can be quite destructive, even.
Anita:	So, how can you know who has God in their hearts and who hasn't?
Mike:	That's exactly the right question to ask. You know them by what they do – the way they behave. It's not so difficult to see who's genuine.
William:	Whoa! Wait up. People can pretend, can't they?
Heather:	Of course they can. But pretending to love is pretty obvious - it's love that counts, not words.

William	OK. But if it's love that counts, you can do that without being a Christian. Not all the people who do good things go to church - or claim to be a Christian or whatever?
Heather:	But if you are going to love you need to be loved. It's basic psychology. Love, to work, has to go around and keep going around. If you weren't loved, you'd soon run dry. To love and keep loving is to bring God's love in, even if it comes through someone else.
William:	Are you saying they have God in their hearts even if they don't know it?
Mike:	Yes, we are. All it takes is an open heart. It doesn't matter what label a person has or whether he or she attends a church. Many people have God in their hearts without realising where the power comes from. Often people become Christians when they see God that has been there all the time - helping them be good, caring, giving people.
Anita:	Why would they do that? I mean, if they've been getting on quite well without knowing God has anything to do with them.
Heather:	For all sorts of reasons - sometimes it's when life takes a dark turn or new things happen in their lives - a new job, going to college—
Anita:	Getting married? ... Are you saying God is already in my heart... our hearts?
Heather:	*(Smiling.)* Most definitely. You do love each other, don't you? God gives you the power to do that.
Mike:	Yes. Are you two going to look for God in you, then?
William:	Don't push it, mate!

They laugh. And the conversation moves back to planning the wedding.

Later on that evening, Anita and William began to talk about the possibility of looking for God in their hearts. After all, they had everything to gain and nothing to lose - apart from feeling a bit daft if God didn't turn out to be real.

Things felt a bit strange to start with. Mike and Heather had just told them to talk to God like they talked to each other - they didn't need any fancy prayers. In the end, just talking to God and asking him to be there got more and more natural until one day they found that they knew he was there. It was like the weight of life had somehow been lifted off them as God took the strain.

Readings:
- Song of Solomon 8:1-7
- John 15:1-11
- Galatians 5:22-25

Questions:
- How much do you accept or expect real happiness to be something that only happens for other people? Have you ever allowed yourself to think that if there is a loving God, he would have the power to transform your life?
- Have you ever been put off Christianity by church people who are just as self-seeking as anyone else? (If you are already a Christian, what do you do about church members who have not opened their hearts to the Holy Spirit? What are the risks to them and others of ignoring them versus the risks of taking action?)
- Why do you think Christians are so keen to pass on the Good News of God?
    - A. Because they need more members to keep the church going;
    - B. Because the bible tells them to (e.g. Matthew 28:16-20);
    - C. Because they want people to be as fulfilled as they are? (Whether or not those people actually join a church is up to them.)
- Can people of other religions have God in their hearts, too, or is the presence of God's Spirit confined to Christians? (If you want to use bible verses in your answer, make sure you do not use them out of context.)

2

God's Ways

Peter, a church discussion group leader, meets up with Tony a few days after a house group. Tony had brought along a new member, Harry, for the first time.

Tony: Hi, Peter. Thank you for talking to us about 'God in our hearts' the other day.

Peter: Thank you for being there, Tony. How'd it go down with Harry?

Tony: Erm... Can I be frank with you?

Peter: Of course you can.

Tony: I mean, you won't be offended?

Peter: I like it when people are honest... and I won't take it personally. If no one ever came back to me on anything, I wouldn't grow in my understanding. And I'd never know if I was way off beam. Politeness gets in the way sometimes.

Tony: Well, you asked about Harry. He's not the romantic sort and, to be honest, neither am I. You see, all this 'God in our hearts' stuff sounds a bit... well too sentimental for us.

Peter: Go on.

Tony: Well, that's it, really. I – we – don't go in for the warm feelings stuff... Can't stand romance films; give me action and less... 'swept off your feet' - less 'I give you my heart'.

Peter: Yeah. I guess 'God in our hearts' *can* sound a bit sentimental.

Tony: Not that there's anything wrong with being sentimental but we're not really people who talk about how we feel much. We're more into active things.

Peter: But to say, 'God's in my heart' doesn't *have* to be sentimental. Perhaps, I could put it another way – use a different metaphor. Jesus tells a parable about him being like a vine and we being its branches; the life in us comes from him. That's, like, more agricultural. Is that better?

Tony: Yes, that's much better. We are the branches that have to bear the fruit – do the useful stuff. Can I tell Harry it's all right to choose his own metaphors?

Peter: Of course you can. That's why the bible has so many different ones... and there's no reason that every generation can't keep coming up with their own...

So, apart from watching action movies what do you and Harry like doing?

Tony: You mean outside work? (You know Harry is an engineer and I work in a medical lab.) I've always got a project or two going; I'm building a pond. Harry likes carpentry. He's making a bench at the moment, I believe.

Peter: I like working with wood, too; the smell of it is lovely and the way the grains go and the colours of the different timbers... Harry and I have something in common, there.

Tony: *(Tentatively.)* Well... not really. You're a natural romantic, aren't you? Smells, colours, beauty. You see, when the bench is finished Harry'll find someone to give it to; he always does. It's making it that matters – the way something comes together – the perfect joint that will take the weight... It's not about how the wood smells.

Peter: You're right, Tony. I am missing something. I'm beginning to understand. So, when it comes to God, for you he's got to be practical?

Tony: Precisely. It's no good him just being there, dwelling in our hearts. He's got to be making something work, doing something... To be honest, love is not a word that I use much. Especially not if it's written with a heart instead an 'o' - Valentine's day and all that.

And when it comes to church, I spent more time in the boiler house than singing hymns last winter. After I'd got that settled down, I often went and made sure the urn was on for coffee rather than go into the service.

Peter: Thank you, Tony. I'm learning. I think I'm going to be much more careful about the way I use the words 'heart', 'love' and 'feelings' in future.

The more I think about it, I don't think the bible ever uses the word 'love' – which it does hundreds of times – without action. God's kind of love has to be something strong and practical to be worth anything, and sometimes there definitely isn't anything sentimental about it – like love your enemies. And 'God so loved the world that he gave us his son to die'...

And no one's going to argue with you persuading the boiler to work or wanting to do the washing up, Tony! Give *me* the worship any day for preference. But, like you say, we're not all the same. I guess God made us that way.

Readings:
- Luke 10:38-42 & John 11:20-28
- 1 John 3:16-18

Questions:
- Being honest, how often do you feel the presence of God within you? Every day? Once a week? Once a year? Only ever felt it once? Never? How much do feelings matter? Can it be different for different people?
- Mary and Martha had differing priorities. How do *you* judge whether what you are, or what you are doing is right in God's eyes?
- Tony expressed his faith in practical ways. In what ways might God be seen in you?
- "'Love' - the noun - has little weight or substance; it can only be truly measured when it becomes a verb - 'loving'". Discuss.
- Are some ways of loving more important than others?

3
Surprised by God

'Have you ever seen God?' asked the atheist of his tour guide. 'All this faith stuff is just in your head. Nobody has those visions that you read about in the bible any more, do they? They were for an age of superstition; one which we've grown out of. This is all just legend.'

The tour guide replied by asking him to look directly at the Mediterranean summer sun.

'You can't do that, it'd damage your eyes,' responded the atheist.

'Well, if you can't look at the sun which God made, how can you look at God, himself?' came the reply.

♦ True that this may be, does the atheist have a point? We don't seem to be hearing much these days of the visions we read about in the bible. Or do we?

The following passage comes from a piece of romantic fiction by Cheryl Terra. The heroine has a lot of negative things to say about the church she grew up in – but somehow the idea of God has been retained. Then she says this:

We spent the rest of the day en route to Jasper. The nice thing about passing Edmonton was that the landscape changed. Up to that point, the world was shades of dusky gold and vibrant yellow, wheat and canola, until it met pure blue skies as far as the eye could see. It was immense and beautiful, a lonely land stretching far past where the eye could see until it met that thin line in the distance that connected the ground to the heavens.

The fields extended past Edmonton for a while, but soon things changed to green. One moment we were surrounded by farms; around the next corner, trees shadowed the train tracks and leggy pines danced as the engine stirred up the air around them. We darted in and out of forests until mountains began rising around us. The world went from green to grey to green again, the colours deeper, the air richer. I was humbled by the sheer enormity of the rugged Rocky Mountains that pierced the sky...

My heart swelled and I nearly cried. The beauty was like nothing I had ever seen. Stone jutted out around us, reaching and reaching far past the heights any man could build himself, tips of white snow meeting the clouds that dotted the cool blue sky above us. There were trees everywhere, thick and dense forests that beckoned me to explore them, to see what treasures were hidden around the trunks of trees older than any person I knew...

I stood still and silent, letting my eyes take in the creation around me. I touched the cross around my neck without thinking. In no church had I ever felt so humbled. No psalm had left me feeling the glory I did in that moment, and no sermon could possibly compete with the whispers of God that flowed through the world He created.

This is what God is, I thought. My mind was clear, the words strong and steady in my head... He was not a set of rules in a book written thousands of years earlier.

God was love... He created beauty, and He had nudged me onto this train in His mysterious way so I could realise that...

I had never felt so certain of anything.

From *Runaway* by Cheryl Terra

In the mid 19th century, Elizabeth Barrett Browning wrote *Aurora Leigh* which includes these words.

> No lily-muffled hum of a summer-bee,
> But finds some coupling with the spinning stars;
> No pebble at your foot, but proves a sphere;
> No chaffinch, but implies the cherubim:
> And, glancing on my own thin, veined wrist, –
> In such a little tremor of the blood
> The whole strong clamour of a vehement soul
> Doth utter itself distinct. Earth's crammed with heaven,
> And every common bush afire with God:
> But only he who sees, takes off his shoes,
> The rest sit round it, and pluck blackberries,
> And daub their natural faces unaware ...

Readings:

- Exodus 3:1-6
- 1 Kings 19:11-12

Questions:
- "...the whispers of God that flowed through the world he created." Have you ever had an experience like the one in Cheryl Terra's story? Can you describe it? You can use any way you like; it doesn't have to be in words.
- If you haven't encountered God in this way - if you haven't had a 'wow experience' - does that matter?
- How would you respond to the suggestion that all 'wow experiences' are a brain chemistry thing that can be demonstrated through experiment? Does this kind of science rule out all possibility of the sense of the presence of God in them?
- After their experience of the presence of God. Moses and Elijah were given a job to do. Might that be true for you, too, even if you don't know what that is, yet?

4
Being Set Free

Jayne is 15 and is a member of the church youth group. The youth leader has just finished telling the group how special they all are. She ends by saying, 'Don't forget, you are – each of you – a special person in God's creation. After the meeting as they wait to be collected, Jayne takes the youth leader to task.

Jayne: Special? There's nothing special about me.

Youth Leader: I mean it, Jayne. You are *all* special.

Jayne: You're always saying that. How can we all be special? There just isn't anything special about me. Just the opposite. I'm not pretty or vivacious like Maddy or clever like Mary. I'm covered in zits - nobody will ever want to marry me. And I'm boring and bad, rotten to the core—

Youth leader: Whoa! Bad?! Rotten to the core?! I mean if I let you off with all the other harsh and untrue things you've said about yourself, I can't let you say you're *bad* and *rotten*. Where does that come from?

Jayne: But I am, aren't I? I mean if you want to be a Christian, you have to know you're a sinner, don't you? Otherwise you can't be saved.

Youth leader: Doing wrong things doesn't make you 'rotten to the core', Jayne.

Jayne: Yeah? Well I envy other people... That's, like, the tenth commandment, isn't it?

Youth leader: Envying Maddy for being pretty or Mary for being clever?

Jayne: Well, I *would* like to be like them.

Youth leader: Are Maddy and Mary perfect? If there's badness in you, what about them?

Jayne: I... I dunno. I never thought about that. Not much, I guess - specially Mary.

Youth leader: But, wouldn't they have to be bad in order to need to be saved, too?

Jayne: I guess they must be, somewhere. But it's hard to see where. I mean they're both pretty cool. Like, Maddy's great-looking but she doesn't make a big thing of it. And Mary's good to me - helps me understand stuff I don't get in class.

Youth leader:	Apart from yourself, how many people do you think of as sinners?
Jayne:	Well, there's Georgina. She's catty and a bully. Then there's Louise – she'd text you any amount of crap...
Youth Leader:	So they're committing sins. Does that make them bad, rotten to the core?
Jayne:	Well, no... guess not.
Youth leader:	So doing wrong things doesn't make them bad people, then. We all do wrong things, Jayne, but God made us and he didn't make us bad. If we don't come clean about our sins and allow God to deal with them then they could corrupt us, but we don't start off bad.
Jayne:	Nah? But I just *am*. I want to be good but I know I'm not. I mean, how am I special? I'm... I suck at times.
Youth leader:	The work God has got to do, Jayne, is not to make a bad girl good but convince you that you are already good. Just let him.
Jayne:	It ain't like that. You don't know how I feel. All I get is that I'm rubbish and need saving.
Youth leader:	I don't think God would say that. Some people might but they're not God. God loves you, right? He created you. Does God create rubbish?
Jayne:	I guess not.
Youth leader:	Dump the guilt, Jayne; God has. You want to be attractive and bright. That's a *good* thing. Have you asked God to bless you with those things?
Jayne:	That's... that's, like... you can't ask God *that*! And besides have you seen me? I mean, come on!
Youth leader:	Yes, I see you and you've got a lot going for you. But, tell me, are the most attractive people always the ones with a perfect appearance?
	What if *God* told you, you were...
Jayne:	Were what?
Youth leader:	Beautiful, bright, desirable?
Jayne:	(*Laughing.*) But he hasn't, has he? Nobody thinks I'm beautiful. That's just daft.

Youth leader:	Don't confuse being beautiful with being pretty, Jayne. Beauty is greater than prettiness. Is that oak tree over there pretty?
Jayne:	Nah. You wouldn't call it pretty, exactly.
Youth leader:	But it's incredibly beautiful, isn't it?
Jayne:	So you're saying I may not be pretty but I can still be beautiful. But I bet you say that to everyone. How can God care about every one of the seven billion people in the world? How can they all be beautiful?
Youth Leader:	Because he's God. He created the universe – all those billions of galaxies billions of light years away – and he created you. So enough of, 'I'm not special,' You are. You have the potential of being like a great oak tree. Think big. Think strong. Think beautiful. You belong to God. Ask him for what you want. Hold your head up high and be the person God made and is making you to be. You may not be Maddy, or Mary but you're Jayne – created in love and bathed in God's glory. That's what makes you beautiful.
Jayne:	No one's ever said nice things quite like that to me before.
Youth leader:	My privilege to be the first then. But I promise you, I won't be the last. Stay close to God and bathe in his glory.
Jayne:	'Bathe in his glory' - I like that. You're, like, poetic, you know that?

Readings:

- Psalm 139:13-18
- Matthew 18:21-22
- 1 John 1:5-10

Questions:

- This discussion is headed, "Being Set Free". What is Jayne being set free from?

- Is the youth leader right? Can we all be special, beautiful even? What *is* beauty?

- Jayne has a low opinion of herself. How do you think she might have come to have low self-esteem? How common is that among teenagers? And among adults?

* What role does bullying play in our image of ourselves? How prevalent is it in schools, the workplace, family or even church? How can we counter it?

* Some people 'fancy themselves' and don't appear to have any problems with self-esteem. How would you respond to them?

* Does God really mean it when he promises to forgive and forget? How can he do that? Is that really true?

5
Flaws, Gulfs, Pits and Crevasses

You ask me to tell you my story. You don't realise how scary that is. It's not that I don't trust you and I know you won't go around blurting it to everyone; you're not a gossip. It's just that I have to admit that I've got great holes in my life. Actually, I'm not so conscious of the critics these days – gossips and bullies and those out to think the worst.

OK, so I'll tell you my story. I guess it began even before I was born because I was getting the message even then that I wasn't wanted. And after I came into the world... well I don't need to go into the details.

For years after I officially became an adult what I told people about myself wasn't my story. My whole life was a lie; I even lied to myself – for years. Years and years of pretending. Pretending to be strong, cool, in control, happy... But none of it was true. Underneath – and not far underneath at that – I was a mess. The thing is, people knew that, and I knew they knew that, but I made out they were wrong about me; I told myself over and over again that those who rejected my job applications, tutors who never bothered to comment on my work, Facebook friends who didn't 'like' me, or people who didn't reply to my emails were the ones who sucked... but me? I was OK. Well, the first bit might have been true; they mostly did suck. I wasn't good at choosing who to associate with. But the second part definitely wasn't – I wasn't the 'me' I wanted people to think I was.

You see, below the surface, I'm a mess. I have great crevasses in places, like those in a glacier. They are deep – so deep they don't have a bottom and are difficult and dangerous to cross. The glacier that's me has lots of snow bridges and, at first sight, you think it's all good but as soon as you venture out the snow gives way and you're scrabbling not to fall in. My unconscious instinct has always been to try and fill up the crevasses or build sound bridges. What you do is that you look for the good things and pretend to yourself that you deserve them and more of them. I looked for the positive things people said here and there and then pestered them for more and more. As a child, I was desperate to cut a nice kid out of the herd and make him or her my own special friend who was not allowed to be a friend to anyone else. Of course, that never lasted – I ended up with no friends at all. And even as an adult I was always manipulating people for attention – cornering them so that they couldn't ignore me. I'd play the 'hard-done-by child' game – whinging and wheedling – and if that didn't work, get angry and 'fly off the handle'.

It all came to a head when I pursued someone on their holiday – I mean literally, not just on social media. He was on holiday with his friends and I just 'happened to turn up' – in the same village in Spain! Of course, he saw through it – who goes on that sort of holiday on their own? I pretended that it was a pure coincidence and then tried to become part of the group, uninvited. He was polite at first but when I persisted he got annoyed. I got angry and he cut me. Told me to get lost – told me to go home. He blocked me on all the social media and black-listed my number. And he was a nice guy. Underneath I knew it was me fooling myself but I had pretended that something was going to come of this. I was rock bottom – only, in my case, I had found neither rock nor bottom.

I flew back to London, packed in my job and disappeared. As a single person, you can easily disappear in London – all you have to do is pay your rent on time by direct debit and no one will notice whether you're in your flat or not. I went out – I wasn't going to return. I was going to have a good time in Soho, get drunk and then jump off a bridge. It would be ages before anyone would miss me – probably not for months, not until my savings ran out. And I took delight in feeling sorry for myself.

I got so drunk I was thrown out of a nightclub by a bouncer, so I bought a bottle of vodka from an all-night off-licence and made my way to the river. I don't remember anything else. Apparently I didn't get to the bridge. I nearly died of alcohol poisoning on the way.

I came to in hospital. My first instinct was to get up and get out but I was too ill and collapsed as soon as my feet touched the floor. Most of the nurses were brusque and efficient but there was this one middle-aged one. She was different. She was the first person to ask me for my story – my true story. At first, I gave her the usual stuff but she just smiled and said, "You can tell me the real story. You see, ten years ago I was where you are, now." The thing is that if you are recovering from alcohol poisoning you don't have much of a leg to stand on if you want to live a lie. She said she had deep pits in her life, only she discovered that there were rocks at the bottom. She said – and no one had ever done this before – she said that if I wanted to look her up after I left the hospital and tell my true story, then I could. And I did; I wanted to know where her rocks came from. And it was from her that I heard about God being a rock.

Very soon I was invited to a meeting of a group of people – every age, posh and not so posh – who all had crevasses underneath. Every single one of them definitely had issues and that was when I truly admitted to myself that I had them too. They were the first people I can ever say really understood me.

I didn't want to be flawed, damaged, but once you admit that you are, you discover that few people are as straightforward as they pretend to be. We could all do with being honest with ourselves. The thing I learned from this group was that God gets in through the gaps. He makes sure there are rocks at the bottom that you can stand up on - they're not bottomless as they have always seemed before - and he's in there with you and you know he will get you up out again. He doesn't fill in the pits or paper over them - he lives in them.

The thing is - with God - it doesn't matter how dark it is, he can still see you. You get to see him when you see what he does in the lives of other damaged people.

I've got friends now - friends who have taught me what God is really about. He's not the person I thought of before - for me, God doesn't live in ancient churches (or even modern ones), heavenly music and coloured pictures of Jesus in robes with children around him. I suppose if I have to have a picture at all - and mostly I don't - it would be the wrecked, abandoned and killed Jesus waiting inside a stuffy tomb with a great big stone against it - waiting for God to break in and raise him from the dead.

That's my story. That's why you'll find me working on the streets with the Street Outreach Programme. Maybe I can help someone else discover that God is there in their pits.

Reading:
- Psalm 31

Questions:
- The storyteller claims, "few people are as straightforward as they pretend to be". Is that a correct assessment?
- In his novel *Angel Pavement*, J.B. Priestly comments about 1930s London: "There was a size, a richness, about London. You could find anything or anybody you wanted in it, and you could also hide in it." Our storyteller here claims a person could disappear in London - would not be missed for months. How easy is it for people to disappear in the world you inhabit?
- The storyteller identifies with a crucified Jesus on the inside of the tomb waiting for his resurrection. Which parts of the Christian story do you identify with most often, if any?
- How hard is it for people to be honest with themselves and others about their faith journeys or lack of them? In what ways do church communities help or hinder in this?
- In Psalm 31, King David is aware of plots against him and he calls upon God. Most of us aren't political rulers with devious enemies setting traps for us. What is it you need to be rescued from? This will be different for

each of us but very few people are lucky enough not to need rescuing from something.

* Psalm 31:14 calls on us to "wait for the Lord". The psalmist recognises that in this waiting we become strong and take courage. God is already with us as we we wait with him for the "day" that is "at hand". (Romans 13:11-12.) Do we find this prospect exciting? If so, how do we pass on the joy of this anticipation to others without sounding judgemental?

6
Finding God in Other People

Colleagues, Josie and Jill, are chatting in a pub after work. It's a noisy place with lots of friendly exchanges. Topics of conversation range widely but somehow Josie gets onto religion, perhaps because she's bored with politics and doesn't want to talk about work or sport... or romance.

Josie: I like the idea of there being something – someone – God – out there and that when we die we go to heaven and all that but how can I be sure it's not all just wishful thinking?

Jill: Just forget it. There isn't a God, Jo.

Josie: How can you know that, Jill? I mean just because you can't see him...

Jill: There just isn't any evidence for him. I mean the scientists have got the world and all that sorted out. You don't need a god to make it work. And we get on perfectly all right without him, don't we?

Josie: Do we, Jill? Speak for yourself.

Jill: Just look at it. There's been more wars over religion than anything else. We're better off without it.

Josie: Yeah. But people fight over everything. I reckon we could do without football for a start. I'd get rid of it for all the tr—

Jill: Now hold on, Jo. Just because there are some hooligans doesn't mean you have to ban the game for everyone.

Josie: And the corruption. Look at the football scandals over the years at the top – the big guy in charge – Swiss wasn't he?. It's all a fiddle.

Jill: That's rubbish! It's not *all* corrupt! Football gives people – sensible people – a lot of fun... and the skill—

Josie: So if football isn't *all* bad, why can't we say the same for religion? Everything has got its bad guys – every country, every walk of life – that doesn't make them all bad...

There are idiotic extremists in anything and everything. It's just...? when it comes to God... I've got this feeling that I'm missing something. It must be great to think there is a God out there who cares about you – forever.

Jill: It's not the same, though, is it? You can go and see Man United – if you can get a ticket – and watch them on the tele. But no one can show me God.

George joins Josie and Jill.

George: Hi guys. What gives? Couldn't help overhearing. Show me God! Now there's a challenge.

Jill: Hi, George. Great to see you. Do join us ... Yeah, that's the point. I can't *show* anyone God. No one can.

George: You sure about that, Jill? If you're interested, Jo, I can suggest how you can connect with God – get to know him... or her, if you want.

Josie: Her!?

George: Why not? God isn't a bloke, is he... or she? God's not human – he's both he and she and neither. She's greater than we can imagine.

Josie: She? I'm all ears, George. You really believe there's a She out there?

George: She or He (or whatever name you want) is more than 'out there', she's 'in here'. *(George taps his chest.)* Let's go and sit down – it's a bit quieter away from the bar.

George takes Josie and Jill over to a vacant table in a corner.

Josie: Go for it, George.

George: *(Laughing.)* I'll do my best. I find the best place to start is to look for God in other people. If Jesus Christ were to come today, rather than 2000+ years ago, what kind of person do you think he (she?) would come as?

Josie: An archbishop... or, no, a holy person from an ordinary background, like, say Mother Theresa.

George: If Jesus is anything to go by, I think we can discount anyone that is already privileged. But Mother Theresa is a good choice. A woman, a foreigner, someone who works with the poorest ... Someone mostly on the outside, someone who a lot of people would totally discount. I doubt he would be a religious leader.

Don't get me wrong, there have been some fantastic archbishops and so on in the history of the world, and, no doubt, we have some good men and women at the top today but Jesus was born poor, on the outside.

Jill: Such as in a stable.

George: Exactly. So you would have to look for Jesus everywhere, especially in the poorest places.

Josie: But Jesus isn't meant to come again like last time, is he? You're not saying that Jesus is walking around today, are you? That's kinda weird.

George: No – not like last time. What I'm saying is that Jesus – God – lives in people – ordinary people – especially those on the outside. You can find him in all whom society leaves out: oppressed people being rescued, prisoners, people in debt, disabled people given new opportunities – education given to those who miss out...

Jill: But hold on. It's not God doing that but people.

George: Yes. But many people say quite categorically that they wouldn't manage to do it – keep giving of themselves without God. The thing is that it's pretty tough in some places and people who work on the front line, so to speak, need the inner resources to deliver.

Josie: Everyone's life can be tough sometimes – you don't have to go looking for it among the poorest.

George: Yeah. True.

Josie: So are you saying that when people say that God has helped them through we have to believe them?

George: I think you have to take them seriously – unless you think they are consciously making it up.

Jill: Like telling porkies? Why do that? I reckon they *think* God has helped them but how can they – and we – be sure?

George: You can't. But somehow the darker life gets, the more people there are who talk about seeing God's light.

So what I am saying, Josie, is that if you really want to try and meet God, you have to take these people's stories seriously. Listen to them.

Josie: And I guess I can start looking in this pub?

George: Everywhere. Perhaps the best place to start is with the people you know and trust. Get talking to someone who says they believe and ask them why? Quiz them.

Jill: Like we're doing you?

George: *(Laughs.)* Yeah. But don't just take my word for it, ask around... Oh, is that the time? I ought to be getting home. It was great to chat and God bless your search for him.

George gets up to leave.

Josie: Hang on, George. What if I wanted to talk to you some more?

George: I could meet you here. Just tell the landlord you're looking for George to talk about God and he'll tell you when I'm about. But you really don't need me. Just remember to look for God in the dark places, that's where She's easiest to see. Tara.

Readings:
- Hebrews 11:32-40
- Romans 15:14-33

Questions:
- Have you met many inspirational people? Who have you been most inspired by and why?
- Do you talk to your neighbours about God? What would need to happen for God to become more a part of your everyday conversation?
- "Christianity is *caught* not *taught*." How much truth is there in this saying?
- Jill, Josie and George enjoyed the social life. Many people do and seek to group together but others are more solitary. Is it essential for Christians to be sociable? Should all Christians hang out somewhere? Does every Christian have to attend a church, even?
- Why do we traditionally call God 'He'? Does it matter if we call God 'She'? What about 'It'?

7

Approaching God

Moira, Fred, Izzy, Richard, Jane and Derek are meeting as a church house group. Jane and Derek have begun to attend church services very recently; neither of them were brought up in church-going families.

Moira: It's great to welcome you, Jane and Derek. How do you find us all at St Whatsit's?

Jane: You're very kind.

Moira: (*Smiling.*) You're allowed to be bold, Jane. Say what you think. We're a bit clubby and not so friendly as we ought to be, aren't we?

Jane: I wouldn't say that. You all know each other and we don't know anyone except you but you can't help that. Derek would have run a mile if we couldn't have stood on the edges a bit, wouldn't you?

Derek: (*Turning a shade of red.*) Yeah, I guess. I'm the quiet sort; I don't really like crowds.

Richard: I get that, Derek. Unlike Fred, here, you won't find me in the pub, like. I ain't no party animal, me.

Fred: (*Pretending to be alarmed.*) You make me sound like a profligate and a drunkard, Richard! I just like company.

Izzy: Now then, boys. The point is, as I see it, it takes all sorts to be a church. Just do your own thing, Derek; it's fine.

Jane: Can I ask something?

Moira: Of course you can, Jane.

Jane: What you all have in common is God, right? He is at the centre when you meet – you do a lot of praying. I get that. But my parents always brought me up not to go round begging and asking for stuff from other people.

But you never stop going: 'God give us this', 'God please can you send your blessings there', 'God mend this' – you're always bending his ear. Doesn't God ever get fed up with that? It seems so... so selfish.

Everyone laughs in agreement.

Moira: It would be if God were a human being. But we do it because that's what he wants us to do. There are times to wait but we have to ask

	and keep asking all the time. Jesus said to ask, seek and knock on his door, not to hang around.
Jane:	But I thought that if God lives in your heart, then he will change you. And he *is* in me – I can feel that already.
Derek:	*(Joking.)* Definitely!
Jane:	Yeah, well it's true..
Moira:	That's wonderful. But how did he get there – in your life?
Jane:	I – we – asked him to come. But really he was there already – I just didn't recognise him before.
Moira:	So he needed asking, right? God always hangs back until we ask. That's his way. He never forces himself on us; how we deepen our relationship with him is always down to us. If we don't ask, we don't get.
Jane:	But surely, if God is God, he knows what we want, what we need.
Moira:	Of course, but he waits until *you* know what you need, admit it to yourself and ask for it.
Fred:	Unlike God, some of us are not the type to hold back,. I just go on and ask.. If there's a sacrament going, count me in.
Derek:	*(Quietly to Richard.)* A sacrament? What's one of those?
Richard:	Sounds threatening, don't it? It ain't really – just a posh Latin word for a blessing, like. They mean Holy Communion, mostly. But any kind of special blessing – grace – can be a sacrament. Don't be put off by the Latin and Greek – it just reminds us that Christianity goes back two thousand years...
Derek:	Holy Communion, the bread and the wine. Yeah. But Jane and I can't take that, can we?
Fred:	Of course, you can, if you want it.
Moira:	Fred!... Officially – technically – you're supposed to do things in the designated order.
Fred:	Yeah. But, in the end, it's between you and God, not you and the rules.
Jane:	I'm confused.
Izzy:	Don't be. *(To Fred and Moira.)* Guys, stop losing God in the details. *(To Jane.)* It's not difficult: it's God and you first, the church and its rules second... The 'designated order' is Baptism first, but God will let you know what he wants you to do, so take Communion if you feel he's calling you to.

Derek: Actually, Jane and I are already baptised because we were christened when we were babies. Isn't baptism the same as christening?

Izzy: Yes. Great. No problem. In our church when you are old enough to understand what it's about you can be 'confirmed' – confirm your baptism... when you're ready. Confirmation's a sacrament, too.

Moira explains Baptism and Confirmation and what Jane and Derek have to do to go about it if they feel called.

Jane: So we have to ask the vicar. OK, I get it. Back to asking again – ask God, ask the vicar...

Moira: *(Laughing.)* Yeah. Everything about God is responding to an invitation. He invites and waits for us to respond. No pressure, though. God is not a salesman wanting to 'seal a deal'.

Jane: But if we *do* want God to do things – for us, for other people, for the world – we have to put pressure on *him*.

Fred: Who, the vicar?

Izzy: Fred!

Jane: (Smiling.) Fred! You know I meant God.

Fred: Yeah. Go ahead and put as much pressure on God as you like. He loves that - he thrives on it.

Readings:
- Matthew 7:7-11
- Mark 5: 21-43

Questions:
- How inclined/disinclined are you to badger God? Why do you think God waits for us to ask?
- Can you tell a story of how God has answered a prayer?
- The woman who touched Jesus disobeyed the Jewish rules (Leviticus 15:25.) which did not prevent Jesus having compassion on her. Bearing in mind that we have rules to enable society to work justly and smoothly, what do we do when our laws, conventions and customs appear to prevent us approaching God?
- Fred and Izzy are not bothered about the 'designated order' of the sacraments. What do you think?
- At one point Jane says she is confused. In your experience, how often does confusion arising from disagreements within the church come between God and individuals seeking to know him?

8

Rainbows

A seven-year-old was being taken on her first visit to a cathedral. Her parents were awed by the huge vault above them, the magnificent stained glass and the furnishings dating back a thousand years. But their daughter was immediately attracted by a modern painting of the parable of the Lost Sheep with the ninety-nine that didn't stray. They were all standing under the span of a glorious rainbow. As she stood gazing at it, she asked, "Why's there a rainbow?"

Her parents looked at one another, each willing the other to supply the answer. As far as they knew, the parable of the Lost Sheep didn't have a rainbow in it. Eventually the mother replied, "Because the artist thought he wanted to put one there."

"But why?" the girl persisted. The rainbow was so central; there had to be a reason for it. She herself had drawn a rainbow to put in their front window at the beginning of the lowdown. It was a way of saying thank you to the doctors and nurses for looking after people. "Is it because Jesus is trying to make that lamb he's holding better?"

"Maybe," responded her father. "The Good Shepherd is about God rescuing those who get lost."

Rainbows in the bible begin with the Noah story. God says:

I'm putting my rainbow in the clouds, a sign of the covenant between me and the Earth. From now on, when I form a cloud over the Earth and the rainbow appears in the cloud, I'll remember my covenant between me and you and everything living, that never again will flood waters destroy all life. When the rainbow appears in the cloud, I'll see it and remember the eternal covenant between God and everything living, every last living creature on Earth." And God said, "This is the sign of the covenant that I've set up between me and everything living on the Earth." Genesis 9:13-17

The rainbow symbolises a covenant – a promise of care. Although the flood devastated the world – an act of frightening destructive power – God wouldn't ever let it happen again. The rainbow becomes a sign of God's promise to look after "everything living on the Earth."

The Old Testament is a process of learning about God – a gradual understanding through the centuries in which it was put together. Those who follow him come to see that the Lord God isn't a fickle god like the old tribal gods that controlled the weather and people's fortunes. As the Hebrew people's idea of God grew in power and glory, so did their belief that God was a God of enduring love for them.

In the New Testament, no one is left outside – Jews and non-Jews are all included; the love of God is boundless. His covenant is with all the Earth.

- Do God's rainbows still appear to people today – his over-arching care, his deep love that is promised into eternity? Is God's promise still in the rainbows? What do you think about such signs in today's world?

Emily Owen believed that God sent her rainbows.

Emily is a young woman who suffers from NF2. This is a terribly debilitating condition that leads to recurrent life-threatening tumours which attach to the nerves, especially the nerves that connect the ears to the brain. These tumours can be taken away but the operation leaves the patient completely deaf. Emily learned, at the age of twenty-one, that if she didn't have the surgery, she would die. We pick up the story after her meeting with the consultant in the hospital in Manchester.

As we drove out of the car park, my eyes turned towards the water pouring down the car windowpane. I could hear rain drumming on the roof. My gaze travelled unseeingly upward until, in the grey sky I saw a rainbow. I stared in wonder. The rainbow was beautiful and I felt as though God had put it there just for me, reassuring me that I wasn't alone. We continued to drive home, and as we sped the 100 miles along the motorway, we saw rainbow after rainbow after rainbow. I have never seen anything like it, before or since.

Despite the grey day, the bad news I'd received, the dread of more brain surgery and a silent future, the rainbows were there. I reached out. And I grabbed them.

Emily Owen, *Still Emily*

Readings:
- Ezekiel 1:28-2:2 (The Message version is wonderful).
- Revelation 4:1-11
- 2 Peter 1:16-19

Questions:
- Have there been any of God's 'rainbows' in your life? How readily do we talk about them?
- How often do we connect God's great glory to his loving care?
- Can we find any beacons of hope in our present world – in both our own communities and beyond?
- How much of your life do you spend trying to dodge the dark bits? Do you trust God to be there in them?

- "Where do the rainbows go when it stops raining?" asked a child. When things get better in our lives, is it harder to see the glory of God? If so, what can we do about it?

9
The Written Word

Derek and Richard, the quiet ones, chat in a corner clutching a cup of coffee after worship while their wives laugh and talk loudly in a larger group leaving them to watch the children as they play happily on a mat with some brightly coloured toys.

Richard: So how's it going then, Derek?

Derek: Fine, Richard. Things are good at home. Coming to worship is a highlight of our week these days. I never thought I'd say that but church is not like a party or the pub. And, I must say, I'm glad Jane is past getting me to nightclubs.

Richard: Nightclubs! I guess I'm way too old for those.

Derek: I never liked them but Jane loved the nightlife. It was when she got big with little Emily that things changed. Then, once, after Emily was born, Jane left me with her and went out again... but she came home early. The nightclub was all full of youngsters, she said. After that she was always looking for things to do, places to go to with Emily.

Richard: That's how she met my Moira. They were both Toddler Group parents. You wouldn't have met me there. Church is about the only place I go outside of work. Given a quiet moment, my favourite thing is books.

Derek: Me, too. Look, Richard, I've been meaning to ask you. I'm tackling the bible but, mostly, I feel lost. I never read any of it when I was a kid. I didn't go to Sunday School or anything. I never realised how much there is in it. To tell you the truth, I don't know where to begin properly. I guess reading it from the first page through isn't quite the thing.

Richard: No. It'd be months before you got to Jesus.

Derek: Years. It's thousands of pages.

Richard: You need a strategy. I'll tell you mine. - but, of course, you don't have to follow mine necessarily. Don't begin with reading chunks without getting an overview. Try at looking at the bible in 3D.

Derek: 3D? Sounds intriguing. How do you mean?

Richard: Period, place and politics. Three dimensions.

Derek:	And, conveniently, three Ps. Go on. What's 'Period'?
Richard:	There are two testaments and sixty-six books in the bible each written and edited at a different period of history over more than a thousand years. It's important you know roughly where each bit of text sits in the grand scheme of things.
Derek:	Yeah. A thousand years!
Richard:	More than. From at least 1000 BC to around AD 120.
Derek:	So where do I find that out?
Richard:	You need a timeline. For the Old Testament, I use one in Charpentier's *How to Read the Old Testament*. I guess the book's a bit old now but there will be things online if you look.
Derek:	I like a proper book.
Richard:	Yeah. So do I. I'll lend you my copy. The New Testament's easier. It was all written in a matter of seventy years. And you can get bibles with this kind of information in.
Derek:	I'll find one. So that's Period. What about Place and Politics?
Richard:	You have to ask where the piece was written and who and what for? For everything the author or editor said, wrote or kept in the bible, he had someone in mind; it is unlikely he thought about people thousands of years in the future much. Occasionally he might but mostly it was meant for the people they knew.
Derek:	What about the end of the world stuff? Isn't that the future?
Richard:	Yes, but take the book of Revelation, for example. The people that mattered were the Christians that were up against it at that time. The nasty people they had in mind were their Roman persecutors. The beast was the Emperor Nero. They wrote it in a kind of code. They weren't thinking of people 2000 years on. They were a small group of a few thousand just trying to survive the immediate persecution.
Derek:	Ah! I get it. Politics. So what you're saying is, when I read it, read it in context.
Richard:	Precisely. Context. Good word. If you haven't got any yet you should read some decent commentaries - and get the bible notes from Veronica over there.
Derek:	I've seen them. I will. But I think I want to do more than just a short passage. When I've got an overview, where should I start?
Richard:	Start with Jesus. It's important that you read all of the bible including the Old Testament through the "lens of Jesus" who

	reveals to us the true nature of God. Begin with the Gospels. Matthew, Mark and Luke have stories in common. Matthew and Luke almost certainly had copies of Mark in front of them. That would make Mark the first Gospel to be written so begin with that. After that, you might like to read most people's favourite bits - the purple passages.
Derek:	Purple! passages? Why purple?
Richard:	Expensive colour only worn by royalty - extra special. I'll tell you what. I'll make out a list of a few to get you started. Get to know those and you're a long way to understanding where the bible is coming from - and where in it you can meet God.
Derek:	You can meet God? Where? In the text?
Richard:	You can see where people down the ages have been inspired by God and why they want to tell their story. When we read, the Holy Spirit in us kind of glows. I know that might sound daft but that's the only way I can describe it.
Derek:	Like when something makes sense. Falls into place.
Richard:	You'll go far! Sometimes what you read just makes perfect sense.
Derek:	That's what I hope for. You lot here have done that for us - me and Jane.
Richard:	Thanks. Thant's the other thing. Before you read, pray. Ask God to help you get what he wants you to hear.

Jane comes across.

Jane:	Hi, Richard. *(Turning to Derek.)* I hope you don't mind but I've just succumbed to Veronica's hard sell and bought a subscription for some bible notes.
Richard:	(Laughing.) It's amazing how often coincidences seem to happen when you open up to God.
Jane:	What's funny?
Derek:	Richard has just! been trying to persuade me to ask Veronica for some notes, too.
Richard	Enjoy!

Readings:
- Luke 1:1-4
- 1 John 1:1-4

- Acts 8:26-40

Questions:
- Derek didn't grow up with a background of bible teaching. Sadly, this is not uncommon. How can those who have been fortunate enough to have done so best help those who are coming new to the Scriptures? What are the dos and don'ts?
- Is Richard right in saying context is very important? If so, why?
- Richard lists some of his favourite passages. Have you any passages in the bible that you find especially difficult and why? How might his advice on looking at everything 'through the lens of Jesus' work in practise?
- How would you answer someone who claimed that the bible speaks of a violent, vindictive and cruel God who has created a flawed people, set them an impossible task, accused them of failure and sentenced them to eternal punishment?
- Richard uses the pronoun 'he' for the writers and editors of the bible because they all were. How much of a problem is this?
- The other chapters in this study look at a variety of different ways of meeting God. Do you find the bible a more important, less important or equally important way?
- Richard claims we can meet God in the text of the bible. Can we meet God in other literature - ancient or of our own time? How might God use the written word in general?

Notes:
1. Charpentiers, Étienne (1981), *How to Read the Old Testament* (SCM Press)
2. Here is Richard's list of his fifteen favourite New Testament passages outside of the four Gospels. There are many inspiring bits of the bible, including the Old Testament. You might like to make your own list and share it with your friends.

   - *Acts 17:22-31.*
   - *St Paul's letters: Romans 8:31-39; 1 Corinthians 13; 2 Corinthians 4:1-6; Galatians 3:27-28; Galatians 5:22-23; Ephesians 3:14-21; Philippians 2:1-11; Philippians 4:4-7; Colossians 1:15-20; Colossians 3:1-4;*
   - *Other letters: Hebrews 11:1-3; 1 Peter 2:1-10; 1 John 4:7-12*
   - *Revelation 21:1-6*

10

Beyond Words

Three long-term school friends meet up after work to catch up on what's new. Jenny's husband, Matt, is making a serious attempt at bible study but Jenny doesn't find it so easy.

Jenny: The trouble with me is that I'm not much cop with words. I'm not a reader. Matt is doing his daily bible stuff but I was never any good at that kind of thing.

Jaz: Me, neither.

Jenny: God seems so kind of, like, words, words, words... You know what I mean. Church is OK if you're into books – if you're not, you kind of... well, get left behind a bit.

Anna: Yeah. But it needn't be like that. I met God at the ballet.

Jaz: Ballet? What? God got tickets for *Swan Lake*?

Anna: It was *Romeo and Juliet*. And no, he was not in the audience but in the dancing, the music and the staging. Don't laugh at me, guys – I'm serious.

Jaz: I never knew you were into ballet, Anna. How did you get to go there? Isn't it, like, really expensive?

Anna: I guess so. I didn't buy the tickets. It was a few years ago now in Germany when I was a teenager. I was doing that exchange thing when you go and stay with a family for a couple of weeks and then their daughter comes back and stays with you.

Jenny: Yeah, I know. I never spoke a word of German – didn't have to because they were, like, brilliant at English.

Anna: Yeah. It was the same with me. They were really different from our family – into all sorts of things and ballet was one of them. I, honestly – and you mustn't laugh at me, please girls – I cried so much I got through half a box of tissues.

Jaz: Tissues! Not chocolates?

Anna: Tissues.

Jenny: Tell us about it, Anna.

Anna: Well, you know how hard Shakespeare in Year 11 was for us?

Jaz: It was, like, torture. But, if I remember, Anna, you got a C in it. Amazing.

Anna:	I did. And it was all down to the ballet. You see a ballet has no words in it. The dancers have to tell the story just by dancing and miming their feelings. The music says it, too.
Jenny:	I can get that. Go on.
Anna:	Well, I never understood what *Romeo and Juliet* was really about. I knew it was about them killing themselves at the end because they came from enemy families. It struck me as bit of a sad kind of love story. But back then, I still thought love was finding your prince and getting him to sweep you off your feet with the final scene being a wedding in fabulous clothes, leaving for a dreamy honeymoon, and then happily ever after.
Jaz:	And it certainly isn't that. You wake up one morning in the cool light of day and find your prince is really a frog. My bloke is a frog - but a nice one.
Anna:	But, the thing is, in that ballet I suddenly *understood* love - what real love is. It's not a romance. I mean, in that ballet, I really got why Romeo did himself in and why. And when Juliet woke up and found *him* dead, she helped herself to the poison, too. Because then that love changed everything; the families realised what idiots they had been and made up... It was then that the penny dropped about God and what real love is about.
Jenny:	Because that's exactly what Jesus did. He loved us so much that it killed him. That's how much God loves us.
Anna:	That's what the bible says. I'd heard it and heard it but I hadn't really got it. Words don't get through to my feelings. The tele's on all day and nobody's really listening to it... well, I don't. And Mrs next door is yelling a constant stream of swear words; it starts with her husband until he leaves for work, then it's the kids until they go to school and, if I've got a day off, I hear her start on the dog - and none of 'em take a blind bit of notice. The world's full of talk and nobody listens most of the time.
Jaz:	But the ballet did it?
Anna:	Yeah. God had to do something, I guess. If it'd been a play, I'd been bored silly. But the dancing and the music - it was something else!
Jenny:	We get the kids to dance sometimes in our church but it's mostly words. The minister likes words.
Anna:	But, now I see it in lots of things. It doesn't have to be dance or music. It can be anything. After that exchange visit I got to look

	more closely at the stained glass windows and learned that they are not all the same. Heidi – my exchange friend – was asking about the stained glass windows we have at St John's. Most of them are boring and kind of flat but there's this window which has Mary holding the dead Jesus in her arms. It isn't big and it's tucked away in a corner but it's about love again. God's in it.
Jaz:	You sound, like, as if you're becoming, like, posh, Anna.
Anna:	No. That's the thing. You don't have to be classy to get art. It's got nothing to do with being educated and that. Look, last year I went to an art gallery and I heard the guides all going about paintings with words, trying to explain about this bit and that bit but you can see most of the visitors don't get it – they're bored. I reckon that if an artist is any good, you don't need words. They say it all in the picture. Ever since that ballet I look and see if I get it. If I don't, I move on.
Jenny:	So you meet God in pictures, too?
Anna:	Some of them. It depends. Sometimes you see the devil.
Jenny:	It's, like, art takes you deep under the surface and says things words can't.
Jaz:	It wouldn't work for me. I'm just no good at words but I'm hopeless at drawing, singing and dancing, too. There's no hope for me, there.
Anna:	But you don't have to be good at *doing* it. It's not about doing it but looking at it or watching it to see if you get what the artist or composer or whatever is saying. We don't have to be great at stuff, ourselves.
Jenny:	Just get it and then, like, cry. Meet God.
Anna:	Yeah. And *then* you know love is real. Really real. And God is behind it all; he was the one who put it there in the artist. All we've got to do is see he's there loving us with his forever real love.

Readings:

- Psalm 139:1-12
- Ephesians 3:14-end

Questions:
- Have you ever been really moved by a performance of music, dance, theatre, fine art, sculpture, etc.? What was it about the particular piece that moved you so much?
- Have you got a favourite stained glass window, piece of music, painting, or any kind of art that you keep coming back to? Is there one that speaks to you of God as it did Anna?
- Prokofiev did not claim to be reflecting the love of God in his ballet and the performers may not have been aware of being a vehicle for God. Does that matter? Can they still reflect God without realising it or even intending it?
- We are all created different. When Gary Lineker was sixteen his teacher wrote in his report that he should spend less time at playing football and more in his academic studies because he would not earn a living at football. Fortunately for him, Gary Lineker knew his strengths and stuck to them. People still say, however, that academic achievement is more important than other skills. Most footballers don't succeed in making a living from their sport and relatively few drama students end up on the professional stage. In the end, it is said, words are more important than anything else for everyone. Do you agree?
- Anna says, "It's not about doing it but looking at it or watching it to see if you get what the artist or composer or whatever is saying." Sometimes society demands that we all discover what we're good at. But what if we're not particularly good at anything? Recently, I watched a performance on YouTube of a teenage singer – she was brilliant – however, one of the comments below was, "I wish I had her talent – I suck at everything. I'm useless." How would you respond to that person?
- Anna says she sometimes sees the devil in a work of art. Is she right? How dangerous can art be?

11

How Big is Your God?

'Far out in the uncharted backwaters of the unfashionable end of the western spiral arm of the Galaxy lies a small unregarded yellow sun.

Orbiting this at a distance of roughly ninety-two million miles is an utterly insignificant little blue-green planet whose ape-descended life forms are so amazingly primitive that they still think digital watches are a pretty neat idea.'

Douglas Adams, So Long and Thanks for all the Fish: The Hitch Hiker's Guide to the Galaxy – Book 4.

Quiz: (Answers on page 46).
1. A light year is the distance it takes light to travel in a year: 9,460,730,000,000 (almost a trillion) kilometres. How far away were the most distant galaxies when they emitted the light that reaches us now?

    A. Around 13 hundred thousand light years.

    B. Around 13 million light years.

    C. Around 13 billion light years.

    D. Around 13 trillion light years.

2. The Sun is a medium-sized star in a medium-sized galaxy (the Milky Way) which contains an estimate of at least:

    A. 100 thousand stars.

    B. 100 million stars.

    C. 100 billion stars.

    D. 100 trillion stars.

3. How many atoms are there in a teaspoon (5 grams) of water?

    A. 500 million.

    B. 500 billion.

    C. 500 trillion.

    D. 500 billion trillion.

4. Approximately how many cells are there in an adult human body?
   A. 30,000
   B. 30 million
   C. 30 billion
   D. 30 trillion

OK. So you get the picture. The creation is unimaginably vast and hugely complex. Today, scientists can look way out into space and, at the same time, discover the tiniest particles that are too small to measure. And the more scientists discover, the more they find to explore. If we believe in a creator God, then we have to believe in a God who made/makes all of this. How big is your idea of God?

> At the beginning, all was formless and empty, and the dark was deep.
> Then the Creator spoke.
> Her Spirit, her Breath, and her powerful Winds, fell upon the chaos.
> There was an explosion of new order.
> The laws of nature came into being, dimension upon dimension.
> Light illuminated the darkness.
> Life and love followed.
> All was wonderful beyond measure.
> Finally, She created a race of people with bodies, minds and hearts designed
> to explore, discern, feel and love all that She had called into being.
> And, then, She, who is all-love,
> touched the people she had made with her Winds,
> so that they, too, grew, knew and spoke.
>
> Even before the beginning, She chose every one of them to become holy and pure.
> She chose them out of love - loved even before they were created.
> She poured into them the power to love as She loves.
> But the people She made abused that power and rejected her.
> Yet her love was undimmed and through that love, She gave of her very Self.
> The Creator emptied herself of her God-power
> and became one of them in time, for a time
> to restore and give new birth to all that She had made.
> She absorbed every anger, heat, hate and blame
> and turned it into love and flawless life.
> Then, at the last,
> She bequeathed them her Breath to lead them to love again,
> the first fruits of an eternal New Creation,
> full of the Winds and Wonders of God.

Readings:
- Isaiah 40:25-31.
- Job 38:1-7.
- Romans 8:31-end.

Questions:
- Douglas Adams labels Planet Earth in the context of the galaxy as an 'insignificant little blue-green planet whose ape-descended life forms are so amazingly primitive...' He's being deliberately provocative here - it's part of his wry humour - but, in reality, how insignificant are we?
- If God created the furthest-flung depths of space, are you too small to be noticed by him? If you don't think so, why not?
- It's easy for us to think of ourselves as autonomous but in reality we are ultra-dependent and intricately interconnected with our environment. Where does God fit into all of this, or would we rather not think about it and liberally apply disinfectant that kills 99% of germs (our microbiome), dead?
- How do you mostly think about God? Where, in the scheme of things, is he located for you most of the time?
- Surely, God is too big to fit into any church. How often do you unconsciously make him small enough to fit yours?
- For you, does the immensity and complexity of the universe make it easier or harder to meet God?

Answers to the quiz:
1. C. The universe is estimated to be 13.8 billion light years old, so, looking at these galaxies, we can see way back to the beginning of things. In that time, however, the universe has continued to expand and these galaxies are now 45 billion light year away!. The expansion is faster than the speed of light, so their current light will never reach Earth.

2. C. But some scientists say as many as 800 billion. The largest known galaxies contain 100 trillion stars.

3. D. Exactly two thirds are hydrogen and one third oxygen.

4. D. An estimated 30 trillion plus another 39 trillion bacteria, fungi and viruses, most of which are essential.

Before You Go...

- Read: Mark 8:22-25.

In this world, we can know God inevitably only in part; let us be forever conscious that our Christian tradition – the traditions of any and all religions are wholly inadequate in their understanding of God. Let us not forget for one moment that, however powerful our experience of him, it is but the tiniest part of the fullness of God.

We journey on. But the glimpses are wonderful when we catch the scintillating reflections of God's grandeur – 'like shining from shook foil' as Gerard Manly Hopkins expresses it in his poem, *God's Grandeur*.

Let us stop, listen, ask and never cease to seek. And may God open our eyes, no matter how many times we have to have the salve of the parable applied.

ACKNOWLEDGEMENTS

I am grateful to Emily Owen and Cheryl Terra for permission to quote from their books. Also to my beta readers who have given me very helpful feedback and without whom I would not have been able to complete this work.

I thank God for them and everything else.

Trevor Stubbs

COPYRIGHT

- Terra, Cheryl: *Runaway*, (Kindle Ebooks. ASIN: B086Q6XMSP)

- Owen, Emily: *Still Emily*, (Sarah Grace Publishing)

About the Author

Trevor Stubbs was born in Northampton, England in 1948 and studied theology in London, Canterbury and Exeter.

He was ordained a priest in the Church of England in 1975.

He has lived and worked in West Yorkshire and Dorset in the United Kingdom, and Australia, Papua New Guinea and South Sudan. He currently lives in retirement in Keynsham, near Bristol.

Trevor Stubbs is married with three adult children and two grandchildren.

For more information about Trevor Stubbs
or to contact him email:
www.tlppress@yahoo.com
or follow him on Twitter: @TrevorNStubbs
or Facebook: revtrev.stubbs

Also available from The Listening People

Disowning the Violence

Tina Stubbs

ISBN 978-1-915288-05-9

Does the Old Testament image of a violent God calling for war, destruction and ethnic cleansing disturb you? If so, you may find this book helpful. Tina Stubbs contrasts the Old Testament understanding of God with that of Jesus and to show that the way we interpret the bible as a whole makes it possible to discount the truth of the destructive and cruel image of God without losing the Old Testament.

The bible tells us what the ancient people thought about God as much as it tells us about God himself. Many horrific acts are attributed to God for which the God we see in Jesus could never have been responsible.

Tina Stubbs shows us how we can disown the violence without disowning the Old Testament.

UK £7.99 / Order from your bookshop or mail <tlppress@yahoo.com>

www.thelisteningpeople.co.uk

Stardust

Trevor Stubbs

Beautifully illustrated by Anna Hewett-Rakthanee

The Bible claims that the light of God seen in Jesus Christ shines in the darkness and the darkness has neither understood it nor put it out. These stories – both profound and light-hearted – direct us towards light and love wherever we may find ourselves.

"This thought provoking and soul-stirring book is one to be read again and again. A beautiful, deep and often breathtaking collection of stories, meditations and reflections." Emily Owen

"Trevor Stubbs gets inside the lives of young people and reminds us of the pain and oddity of those years as we sort out what really matters. He has a gift for narration and a wonderful way of 'dancing with words'." Mary Cookson

Hardback: ISBN 978 0-9550100-9-5   UK £17.99

Paperback: 978-1915288004   UK £12.99

Order from your bookshop or mail <tlppress@yahoo.com>

Proceeds from the sale of books published by The Listening People are used to support street children in Juba, South Sudan or other charitable purposes.

www.ingramcontent.com/pod-product-compliance
Lightning Source LLC
Chambersburg PA
CBHW012252300426
44110CB00040B/2596